Michigan Waters

Concept and Design: Robert D. Shangle
Text: Louis Cook

First Printing January, 1981
Published by Beautiful America Publishing Company
P.O. Box 608, Beaverton, Oregon 97075
Robert D. Shangle, Publisher

ISBN 0-89802-327-0

Contents

Introduction 5

The Ones That Didn't Get Away 7

Mayday! 9

Not By Bread Alone, But Bread Helps 16

Starboard Tack! 20

The Worse It Smells, The Better It Works 24

Throw Out The Life Line Across The Dark Wave 59

This Is Noah 63

A Window To The World 67

Photo Credits

INTRODUCTION

Michigan was very young when Henry Wadsworth Longfellow sang the Song of Hiawatha. But even then the Great Lakes had excited the imaginations of people throughout the civilized world, five mighty inland seas making up the largest body of fresh water anywhere. Michigan is the only state bordering on four of them: Michigan, Superior, Huron and Erie. Only Lake Ontario does not lap its shores.

With 3,288 miles of coast line, Michigan touches on more water than any state except Alaska. (Hawaii has a long coast line, but the extent has never been measured exactly.)

From Isle Royale, far out in frigid Lake Superior, to Monroe on Lake Erie and to Benton Harbor on Lake Michigan is the biggest, bluest, most pure collection of water molecules, two atoms of hydrogen to one of oxygen, on Planet Earth; a glorious playground for boaters, swimmers and fishing enthusiasts; a source of drinking water for great cities, a supply for making steel and autos. It is a joy when it is serene and one of the most terrible expanses of water when aroused.

That's not all. Minnesota makes a good deal out of its 10,000 lakes, but Michigan has 11,000, ranging from the largest, Houghton, in the center of the Lower Peninsula with 30 square miles, to tranquil ponds where bass jump and water lilies undulate. Even Michigan's groundwaters are rich in minerals valuable to the chemical industry.

There are dozens of rivers . . . the Au Sable, the Saginaw, the St. Joseph, the Grand, the Raisin, the Pere Marquette, the Muskegon, the Boardman, the Looking Glass, the Tittabawassee, the Menominee, the Paw Paw, the Rifle, the Au Gres; a big mouthful of names reflecting the romantic history of the state from Indian beginnings through the French and British eras to the American.

Some are swift and tumultuous, racing down to the Great Lakes over rocks and gravel. Some are serene and tranquil, winding through quiet valleys where Holsteins graze and fragrant peppermint bends. And there are brooks and rills where brown trout lurk, and boys and girls lie on their stomachs on still afternoons to watch minnows dart.

Water wells up from the ground all over Michigan. The famous mineral spring at Northville once featured prominently in the Barney Google comic strip. Noxage, it was called, and people of southeast Michigan still pull over and fill their plastic gallon jugs from it. Knocks Age . . . get it? Its fans swear that it does.

Probably the best known these days, however, is Big Springs at Manistique, in the Upper Peninsula. It is fed from 20 springs and is colder than a well digger's knees. A penny dropped into its sparkling, deep-blue water can be followed all the way to the bottom 45 feet down. Kitchitikipi is the Indian name. Try it.

In Michigan the treasure of fresh water is taken for granted by most. Yet the city planners make a solid case that it is not land and food, but water that is going to shape the megalopolises of the future. Detroit will likely be the center of a super-city stretching some day from Buffalo, N.Y., to Peoria, Ill.

Already the irrigation pumps in Arizona and California are lowering the water tables to dangerous levels, and brine is seeping in. The reservoirs from Connecticut to Pennsylvania have been running low for 20 years, and diners in New York City restaurants have to ask for a glass of water. The inter-state arguments over who shall have how much from the trickle of the Colorado River are growing in intensity. The Arab emirates are seriously considering towing icebergs from the North Atlantic to the Red Sea. Desalinization of sea water is resorted to increasingly, by expensive and difficult processes.

Michigan's greatest richness is not the navy bean from the Thumb, or the Traverse City cherry. It is water.

THE ONES THAT DIDN'T GET AWAY

There is general agreement among "compleat anglers" that Lake St. Clair, in southeastern Michigan, is the greatest fresh-water fishing ground in the world. From small perch to mighty muskellunge it teems with a great variety of fish. On any good day, Strawberry Island at the outlet of the Clinton River is ringed with anglers. And where the St. Clair narrows down to the Detroit River the channel is thick with trollers for pickerel, also known as walleyes. It is a mystery to fishers how a walleye can see where it is going, but there is no doubt it has great peripheral vision.

Lake St. Clair is a local phenomenon, however. Commercial fishing became a source of profit in the Great Lakes surrounding Michigan as early as 1833. For decades it ranked a close third to lumber and agriculture. In 1860 there were 32 fishing companies in Mackinac County alone. Whitefish, lake trout and perch were the principal catches.

Commercial fishing suffered heavily from the migration of the sea lamprey up the St. Lawrence River to the Great Lakes. They are mean little beasts, Michigan's piranha, that attach a sucker-like mouth to bigger fish and drain their lives away. Their depredations have been controlled by chemicals, and the trout and the whitefish are beginning to come back.

But not yet in the numbers that once brought fleets of fishing boats onto Lakes Michigan and Superior, especially in the Beaver Island area. Storms sent them chugging to harbor, and there are many stories of lost crews, and breathless moments charging the waves at their peak in order to ride over the sand bars guarding the harbor entrances. Difficult though it was, fishing was independence and a living.

Today, the only major center of commercial fishing left in Michigan is at Leland, on the northwest coast of the Lower Peninsula. At "Fishtown," with its nets strung out to dry and the sturdy fishing boats nosed into its piers, one can see how it used to be. One fisherman could bring in 3,000 fish a day a century ago.

In 1965 a new era of Michigan fishing began with the introduction by the state of coho salmon from Washington, Oregon and Alaska. Four-inch smolts were planted in Lakes Michigan and Superior. They and their progeny have spread all the way to Lake Erie and up the major rivers, creating a new sports industry. Charter boat operators. Bait and tackle shops. Sellers of foul weather gear, boats and outboard motors. The salmon widow has become as forlorn as the golf widow and the deer widow, except when she joins the fun, too, as she often does.

The arguments about the best table fish taken from Michigan waters will never end. Whitefish rate high, as do the more caloric lake trout. Pickerel are taken from fast, cold water, and are delicious broiled or baked.

And there are the smelt fans, who dip up the tiny silver slivers by the pailful during the spring runs on the streams running into the lakes. Deep-fat-fried, they are crisp and sweet. Bluegills are the supreme breakfast fry, closely pushed by smallmouth bass.

Yummy.

MAYDAY!

The Great Lakes embracing Michigan are famous for their glorious sunrises and meditative sunsets, studies in serenity and beauty for thousands of musers and photographers. But when the temperatures drop in the fall and the wind rises in the northwest . . . look out.

From the tragic voyage of the Griffin in 1679 to the foundering of the Edmund Fitzgerald in 1975, the distress cry has rung regularly over the storm-tossed waters. The records from the early years of sail are spotty, but the best estimate puts the number of wrecked ships around Michigan at about 6,000: 40 percent off the Lake Huron coast, 35 percent off the Lake Michigan coast and the remainder off the Lake Superior coast. They are concentrated around Thunder Bay, Munising Bay, Isle Royale and the Straits of Mackinac, where the Griffin is believed to have gone down, bound for Niagara with a load of Robert Chevalier de la Salle's furs.

Modern weather forecasting, radar, radio direction-finding, more powerful engines, better construction and better-trained crews have improved the odds for ships on the Great Lakes. Nevertheless, the Edmund Fitzgerald foundered with all 29 hands in Lake Superior on Nov. 10, 1975. With no survivors, what happened is conjecture, but apparently the 60-knot winds loosened her hatch covers, and she nosed into a 30-foot sea and dove to the bottom, her propellers still turning.

A storm of similar intensity broke the Carl D. Bradley in half in northern Lake Michigan on Nov. 19, 1958, while the ship was on the way to her home port, Rogers City, with a load of limestone. There were only two survivors of her crew of 35.

The memory of the Edmund Fitzgerald will linger on in a folk ballad composed shortly after its loss. The other disasters are not remembered as well, but many were worse. Three vessels sank and 67 sailors drowned in the Armistice Day storm of 1940. But the meanest storm in

*Between adventures, watercraft rest quietly
at Traverse City's Harbor West.*

*The unspoiled wilderness of Isle Royale
beckons hikers and naturalists.*

the known history of the lakes was the howler that hit on November 7, 1913, and lasted until November 11.

The storm was reported over Minnesota in time to send out warnings, but the ship captains were under heavy pressure to make the last runs of the season. Besides, the early warnings predicted 38-mile-per-hour winds and blowing snow, enough to worry about but no worse than many other storms the masters and their crews had experienced.

But the winds built to 90-miles-per-hour, and many struggles for survival began. The most remarkable escape was probably that of the 24 men aboard the ore carrier L.C. Waldo, out of Two Harbors. One mighty wave sheared away her pilot house and cabins. The captain and the mate dived down a hatchway and, with no lights or steering wheel, set a broken stool by the hand-powered auxiliary wheel. They steered by lantern light and a compass salvaged from a life boat, and almost made it to an inlet between Gull Rock and Keweenaw Point, grounding on a reef. The ship held together, and the men survived by burning cabin furniture in a bathtub two days and nights.

The James Carruthers and the Hydrus were lost with all hands. The Carruthers was only six months old, Canada's largest and newest laker, 550 feet long and 48 feet abeam. Also only a year old was Lightship No. 82 in Lake Erie. The lightship's captain, Hugh Williams, left a message for his wife on a door panel: "Goodbye, Nellie, ship is breaking up fast."

At least 251 men died in the storm, and 12 ships were lost. Telephone and telegraph lines were down; shore people did not realize the extent of the tragedy until bodies began washing up on the Canadian shore at Goderich, Port Edward and Port Franks.

Bud Goodman, writing in the old Detroit Times when the Bradley went down, referred to the surviving wives as "the widows of the wind." An apt description.

The Great Lakes keep their secrets well. Superior is 1,333 feet in places; Lake Michigan, 925; Lake Huron, 725; and Lake Erie, 62.5 feet. Lake Ontario gets down to 802 feet. For the most part the sunken ships lay undisturbed, until diving equipment became sufficiently sophisticated to permit deep-water exploration.

The French oceanographer Jacques Cousteau and his crew recently visited the Edmund Fitzgerald, after exploring the U.S.S. Hamilton, sunk during a Lake Ontario squall in 1813. The Hamilton is resting on the bottom in 300 feet of water completely intact, including a figure-head of a young girl.

Marine archeologists are studying some gems of old ship-building brought up from the wreck of the Indiana, a 350-ton wooden-hulled ship that sank in Lake Superior in 1858. It had one of the earliest steam engines on the lakes. The 12-foot-high boiler, single-cylinder engine and ten-foot propeller have been shipped to the Smithsonian Institution in Washington, D.C., for cleaning and study. The propeller was an early example of the screw propulsion used in modern shipping.

The America, sunk off Isle Royale in 1928, still has its steam distribution center intact, with valves working. The Monarch, lost in 1906, still has its cargo of paper-manufacturing machinery. The Pewabic sank in Thunder Bay following a collision in 1865, and is still laden with 267 tons of pure copper and 175 tons of iron ore. Scuba divers are lured by tales of ships' safes full of money and jewels, and holds full of silver ore. The principal findings, however, have been copper ingots, anchors, name plates, whistles and marine bric-a-brac.

Detroiters still occasionally find copper spikes in the Detroit River near the Belle Isle bridge, where a yacht built for Abraham Lincoln was burned at her moorings when she became unseaworthy. President Lincoln never sailed on it. It was turned over to the U.S. Navy as a patrol boat at the outbreak of the Civil War.

Preserving Michigan's underwater treasures has become a problem with the development of scuba diving, which already has resulted in the loss of ships' gear and documents. The Michigan Underwater Salvage Committee has nominated 218 square miles in the neighborhood of Munising Bay and another 500 square miles near Alpena as the state's first underwater preserve.

The Michigan Legislature has recently considered establishing an underwater park similar to those already offered in Tobermory, Ont., and along the Florida Keys.

Eventually these evidences of the fury of the storms of the Great Lakes will have to be protected. And when the weather service posts gale warnings and small boat advisories . . . believe them.

Lonely winds keen in the sedge at Ludington State Park.

Nature's way, green pines waiting their turn to join trees of yesteryear mouldering in the Pigeon River.

NOT BY BREAD ALONE, BUT BREAD HELPS

For centuries in western civilization the miller and the millwright were necessary and respected members of the community, and the miller's daughter was often celebrated as of surpassing beauty and an inspiration to poetry. Each early Michigan community had a mill, or access to one within a day's wagon journey, and many of them exist still, although for the most part their wheels turn free and the big stones are silent.

They are beautiful places, with serene mill ponds, mills with stones and carefully hand-crafted wooden gears still intact. In an energy-nervous era there have been suggestions that they be converted to electricity generation, although the return would be small. Several dams for electrical power generation exist, including one at Bellevue, but their turbines are no longer working.

The mill at Manchester, in lower Michigan, still grinds feed for cattle and chickens. Until recent years the mill at Hodunk was active for the same purpose.

The Clifton Mill near Romeo, north of Detroit, ground bread flour as recently as 1974, although it was having difficulty getting the hard red wheat needed for bread flour. Michigan wheat is chiefly soft wheat used in pastry making.

The old techniques were used. The mill stones were kept separated to produce nutty graham flour, the coarsest grade. Closer together, the stones turned out whole wheat flour. Set tight, the stones pulled out a natural-food-lover's dream, a fine tan flour similar to standard white

16

flour, but with the husk and sprout in the finished product. There is nothing quite like bread made from it.

Clifton Mill began turning in 1810. There are others in Michigan equally venerable, but there is no demand for the product that once supplied every table in the state. Modern millers ply their trade in anti-septic places to the west, carefully measuring out vitamins to replace those lost in the modern flour-making process. That's progress?

Calm, like a soothing hand, quiets the water at Les Cheneaux.

A lone canoe plies the stream that flows from Chickenbone Lake
to McCargoe Cove, on Isle Royale's north shore.

STARBOARD TACK!

Whatever one's favorite pastime, there is an inexorable urge to be the one who does it fastest. People race autos, airplanes, trains, snails, frogs, horses, turtles, dogs and carrier pigeons, among others.

And they race boats of all descriptions, from tugboats to ocean liners, Gold Cup unlimiteds to outboards, auto ferries to ore carriers. But the fiercest, most cut-throat competition is between racing sailors, with whom the Great Lakes abound—especially Lake St. Clair, not one of the Great Lakes, but a reasonably large expanse of shallow water between Lakes Huron and Erie.

Sailors pride themselves on being one with wind and wave, moving about on the waters without any help except from the wind and their own skills. They have to stay vigilant or they will wind up on the rocks of a lee shore. They are in the main polite, helpful and respectful of the people in the next boat, be it sail or power.

But when it comes to racing a sailboat, both male and female sailors undergo an abrupt change of personality. Every opponent is their mortal enemy. To get their names on a paltry traveling cup they will suffer dismasting, collision, tattered sails and spending hours being tossed around in a life-belt on stormy waters, awaiting rescue.

A sailor has right-of-way on the starboard tack. When a half dozen racers are boiling in to round the buoy marking a leg on a racing course, they are all bellowing "starboard tack," whether they are on it or not. A favorite ploy is to hold the mainsail over on the starboard tack by hand, to gain a few precious seconds.

Racing sailing has become complicated by the introduction of so many new designs. Thirty years ago the Star boats, the 110s, the 120s and the Lightnings were popular classes. Lightnings are still around, but they have been supplemented by little Thistles, in-between Cal 20s,

Ventures, Catalinas, larger Ericsons, and a host of other new designs big and little.

There are enough Thistles, Cal 20s and Lightnings, as well as Flying Scots, Snipes and Mariners in Michigan waters to put together separate classes of racing sailing. But often the racers mix it up, with faster boats accepting handicaps. The greatest coup for a sailor is to come in first in time ahead of handicapped boats.

Successful racing sailing calls for all manner of elaborate boat gear, subject to collapsing at embarrassing and critical moments . . . boom vangs, Cunninghams, whisker poles, spinnaker rigging, mast rakers, adjustable back stays, pad eyes, Genoa tracks, trapezes and other esoteric gadgets.

It also calls for stealthy cunning to prevent an opponent from stealing your air and leaving you becalmed to leeward, incredible gall in forcing an opposing boat to give way, and a sixth sense in figuring where the wind is and will be, and how tight one can sheet in a 180-degree Jennie without pulling the shrouds out of the chain plates.

The race that excites Michigan imaginations most is the 235-mile yearly event from Port Huron to Mackinac Island. The races began in 1925, sponsored by the Bayview Yacht Club of Detroit. They are not the place for the 20-footers to mix it. The trek up Lake Huron is subject to fierce weather, and there are not many places to hide along the coast in the event of a blow.

The daddy of them all, however, is the Chicago to Mackinac race, begun in 1898 by two sloops and three schooners from the Chicago Yacht Club. Big Bill Thompson, later mayor of Chicago, won that race three times in succession, setting a record of 31:24:06 for the 333 miles that endured many years. It is the longest fresh-water sailing classic in the world.

The cool descent of shadow calms Big Stone Creek in Wilderness State Park.

Oarsmen work out near the Detroit Boat Club, the oldest rowing club in the country.

23

THE WORSE IT SMELLS, THE BETTER IT WORKS

Next to devotees of fishing, the greatest defenders of their particular method of pursuing sport are deer hunters, who have resorted to black eyes and bloody noses in defense of .30-.30s, .30-'06s, magnums, buckshot and solid shot. But they are namby-pambies compared to the adherents to dry flies and wet, spawn bags and night-crawlers, sponge-rubber spiders and fat-head minnows.

The big muskellunge are probably best taken with plugs and spoons and a gadget known as The Believer, which is a variation of a casting plug. Cohos and steelhead trout rise to spoons and plugs. The Pikie Minnow plug is popular for several varieties of large fish.

Pickerel are angled for with wads of night crawlers, either trolling or drifting. Bags of spawn excite steelheads and Cohos. Bluegills require the simplest equipment: a bamboo pole will do, or just a length of willow cut from a nearby copse, with a redworm and bobber. Northern pike, some of the best eating anywhere, baked with onion dressing, are not often sought in Michigan waters for some reason, but they are present in quantity, weighing up to 20 or 30 pounds. They are netted on spoons, either by trollers or by hardy souls who venture into inland lakes hip-deep in the early night and cast into the lily pads where the big ones move in for darkness feeding.

Another prolific species that is without honor in Michigan is channel catfish, much respected on the Missouri and Mississippi Rivers. They grow to monstrous size and are good eating for those who take the trouble to create the proper bait, which is doughball. Bullheads, browns

A day of lily pads and fleeing clouds at Hartwick Pines State Park.

The way it was when the lake trout ran thick:
Fishtown at Leland on Lake Michigan.

A pale birch contemplates its reflection as the
year dies at Stewart Lake.

"I must go down to the sea again . . . and all I
ask is a tall ship and a star to steer her by."

The steel hand of winter, clenched, on the
McLain State Park Lighthouse.

A new day breaks with a glad shout, at Stoney
Creek Lake in Macomb County.

30

The Tawas Point lighthouse on Lake Huron
still sends a gleam across the waves.

Powerboats have churned the Detroit River since
the days of racing king Gar Wood.

The Ambassador Bridge is Detroit's graceful link
to its Canadian neighbors.

Bitter cold and ice crunch as the Coast Guard cutter
Mackinaw clears a path for the freighter Presque Isle.

Generations of men come and go, and white caps
roll the centuries away on Lake Huron.

35

Star-studded entertainment abounds each summer
aboard the Chesaning Showboat, on the Shiawasse River.

Whatever the fury of Lake Huron, the harbors of
Les Cheneaux offer sanctuary.
(Following page) A quiet moment between winter storms
on the Au Sable River.
(Second following page) Hurrying, hurrying, a mighty
rush of silver down Wagner Falls.

Another of a millennium of autumns hushes the Rifle River.

*Incongruous amid serene surroundings, the
Presque Isle lighthouse awaits fall storms.*

A brooding moment in the dying day, the sun sinks
over Lake Michigan near South Haven.

The Presque Isle River tats its own lace as it falls
toward Lake Superior.

43

Winter on the Au Sable, and deer track whispering through the wilderness.

44

A rocky crag holds out against Lake Superior . . . for a time.

Man's proud challenge to wind and wave is the Mackinac Bridge.

46

*Ducks and sailors find peace from Lake St. Clair on Black Creek.
(Following pages) With spinnakers blossoming in the light air,
the Mackinac racers set out from Port Huron.*

Dark clouds hang ominous over Lake Superior at
McLain State Park. Sailor, beware.

Upper Tahquamenon Falls, Upper Peninsula

Joe Kinnebrew created the fish ladder at
Grand Rapids, a major sculpture.

A golf-ball-eating water hazard lies in wait at
Stoney Creek golf course.

Rocky shoreline of Copper Harbor is serene
despite its cragginess.

The fireboat Curtis Randolph sprays a salute to downtown Detroit.
(Following page) Slowly, slowly the Hersey winds past Reed City,
through autumn's glowing majesty.

and yellows, are a homely fish with a hide that has to be stripped off with a pair of pliers. But they are delicious fried in corn meal, and abound in the smaller inland ponds and lakes. They are suckers for a hook imbedded in doughball, too.

A more sophisticated sport is drifting a Royal Coachman fly down a fast stream in pursuit of rainbow and brown trout. Tom Opre, the Detroit Free Press's outdoor writer, believes Michigan has the best fly fishing east of the Rocky Mountains and claims he is seldom disputed.

There are those who consider dangling a doughball in front of a catfish one of the more esoteric forms of angling. The creation of a proper doughball is a high art.

One popular method is to mix grated cheese, the more toxic the better, with flour, water and cotton. The cotton holds the stuff together on the hook. The whole nauseating mixture is then put into a can and buried in the back yard. Baking powder cans are preferred, with a little of the powder left in the bottom to do its heady work.

About two weeks of warm weather are required to bring the mixture to proper rancidity. The can is dug up, and it's off to the nearest pond or stream. It is best to bait the hook holding it downwind, but the doughball beats using aged chicken entrails, which catfish and bull-heads also find entrancing.

(Previous Page) Yesterday's runabout queens rest in still water at an antique boat meet at Algonac.

THROW OUT THE LIFE LINE ACROSS THE DARK WAVE

Since the Fort Gratiot lighthouse was built at Port Huron in 1825, Michigan's lighthouses have had a fascination for tourists, artists and boaters, from those rowing out for a mess of perch to big lakers bringing taconite to the smelters of the lower lakes. Some are fairly homely structures, but most are graceful cylinders rising into the crystal sky like a finger of God, serene, lonely, children of the wind.

The life of lighthouse keepers has been more lonely and dangerous than romantic until recent years. According to the U.S. Coast Guard there are 675 lights on the Great Lakes, not counting lighted buoys. But of Michigan's 75 lighthouses, only four have personnel stationed on them. The rest have been abandoned or have had their equipment automated so they need be visited only for occasional inspection and maintenance.

As recently as 1966 there were 40 manned lighthouses on the Michigan approaches to the four Great Lakes the state abuts. The only ones still requiring personal attention are at Eagle Harbor, Two Rivers, Point Betsie at Frankfort, and Keweenaw, far up in the frosty tip of the Upper Peninsula that juts out into Lake Superior.

Manning the lighthouses was undertaken by the Coast Guard in 1939, when the service merged with the old U.S. Lighthouse Service. Working the Stannard Rock installation, furthest from land of any American lighthouse, was for years considered the loneliest task in the nation. Stannard guards the approaches to Marquette and Duluth, Minn., far out in Lake Superior, 45 miles from Marquette.

And the dawn comes up like thunder across Lake Huron
at Harrisville.

A bright patch in a forbidding winter landscape,
the Grand Haven Light glows in Grand Haven State Park.

Almost as isolated is the Rock of Ages light, three miles off the west end of Isle Royale, the most powerful light in the Great Lakes, with four and a half million candlepower. Its foundation is a pier of concrete inside a steel cylinder, topped by a 130-foot brick tower.

Stannard and Spectacle Reef lighthouses are probably the best known landmarks among Michigan lights. Both were started in 1870 by Major O.M. Poe, who later built the Poe Lock at the Soo. Spectacle Reef light is near the Straits of Mackinac, and presented the same problem as Stannard—building something that could endure the strong currents and the fierce winters in open waters.

For many years they presented eerie sights to the keepers venturing out to start the lights in early spring. They were often solidly encased in ice that mounted to the very lights, and entrance could be gained only by chiseling through ice to the massive doors in the bases. Many other lights were almost as well known: Split Rock on Lake Superior, Little Sable and Big Sable and White Shoal on Lake Michigan, Marblehead on Lake Erie, and the Detroit River lighthouse.

All were built to last and they have, with the exception of the Fort Gratiot lighthouse that was washed away a few years after construction, and had to be replaced. The prettiest is probably the graceful cylinder of the old Presque Isle light, built in 1838 on a lonely spit angling out into Lake Huron. With its walk-in fireplace in the keeper's quarters, it has not changed greatly since the time of its last tender, who was appointed by President Lincoln. It was abandoned in 1870, when a new light was built north of it closer to Presque Isle Harbor. For decades it had been the only navigation guide between Port Huron and the Straits of Mackinac, the salvation of lumber schooners and the early ore carriers. In recent years it has been a private residence. It is probably the most photographed of Michigan's lighthouses.

For many years the only lightship on the Great Lakes was the Huron, anchored off Port Huron. It is no longer in service, a relief to the crews that rode out wild storms in the ship. During the Great Storm of 1913 the Huron dragged its massive anchor and barely survived.

The lights still shine through the stormy nights. And although radar and LORAN and radio direction-finding have taken over much of navigation, there is still no substitute for that flash of light through the rain and driving snow that tells a sailor exactly where he is.

THIS IS NOAH

Every radio and television station in Michigan has a devoted group of listeners and lookers, but none as specialized and avid for information as those who tune in daily to KEC63, the voice of the National Oceanic and Atmospheric Administration in lower Michigan.

It is called Noah, from its acronym, NOAA, an apt informality honoring the man who was the first known weather forecaster, predicting 40 days and nights of rain with Biblical precision. Noah had a little divine help, of course, while the meteorologists of NOAA have to rely on less precise mechanisms of cold fronts, high pressure areas, and lake water levels.

Noah operates at a mere quarter of a kilowatt—far less than many radio amateurs employ in table-top rigs. It transmits on a frequency of approximately two meters, giving it a limited range as well as limited power. But it is the last word on the weather brewing, not only on the lakes but also on southern Michigan farmlands, a curious combination of nautical information and advice to farmers on what the morning dew will be like and when the temperatures will be dangerous for cattle.

There is something endearing about Noah. Its announcers are not professionals, and the news it brings is delivered in accents ranging from nasal twangs through southern drawls. The conversation from Noah is a welcome relief from the pear-shaped tones of commercial broadcasting.

Occasionally there is a little whimsy on Noah. One of its announcers occasionally dwells on the fact that Noah's antenna is mounted "on a tall building in Southfield." Another embellishes this on occasion by remarking the antenna is "a tall tower on a tall building in Southfield." This is about as far as Noah goes in whimsy, however. The rest is inadvertent, as happens when a meteorologist struggles with the pronunciation of Ashtabula, which often comes out Ashatabula.

Michigan's waterways have something for everybody...waves lapping rocks near Fayette ghost town...

gulls and ducks...colorful sailboats pulled up on the sand...the thrill of a nibbler considering the bait...

Unless Noah has something hot in the way of weather information, such as a squall coming up the Detroit River or a small craft advisory for Lake Huron, the messages are taped for repetitive delivery. Often two tapes are transmitted simultaneously, confusing those not familiar with the operation. Old hands, however, can follow whichever conversation is of the most interest to them.

The transmissions would appall professional broadcasters. The backgrounds often include babies crying, children arguing, trucks going by and aircraft taking off. Occasionally one hears a tea kettle whistling, or a vacuum cleaner.

But boaters follow the transmissions carefully. Most of them have special radio receivers in their homes or on their crafts tuned to Noah. It is possible to receive the station on conventional all-wave radios that dip into the two-meter range, but the sure method is to own a special receiver that holds to the assigned frequency with crystal-controlled oscillators.

Noah broadcasts around the clock. Its friendly voices let freighter captains know when the west winds on Lake Erie have piled up the shallow waters on the east shore, leaving the channels around the Islands and Toledo dangerously low in water level. An advisory for small craft means that winds have freshened to 25 knots or more, or will soon, and it is dangerous to venture off-shore.

Noah's headquarters are the meteorological office at the Detroit Metropolitan airport. For all of its humble nature, it has at the most saved many boaters, professional and amateur, from putting themselves in bodily danger; at the least it has saved them from a very uncomfortable day on the water. Noah is the boaters' friend.

A WINDOW
TO THE WORLD

All day and all night, from the breakup of the ice in early spring until the iron fist of winter clenches on the lakes and rivers, the long drone of the passing signals from the whistles of the big ships rolls through sunny days and crisp nights. One blast: I am directing my course to port. Two blasts: I am directing my course to starboard.

The parade of shipping is hypnotic to those who live within sight of it, and thousands do. Binoculars or a big brass telescope are standard equipment in their homes along the Detroit, St. Clair and St. Marys rivers, the Straits of Mackinac, the Frankfort bluffs and many other locations.

Soon they begin to recognize the distinctive stacks of the lakers . . . The Browning Lines, black, red and white stripes; Canada Steamship, solid red at the bottom, black at the top, white in the center; Bradley Transportation, black with a big "L" on grey; Cleveland Cliffs, a big red "C" on solid black; the Ford fleet, a yellow band at the bottom with the familiar Ford signature in white on black at the top; Standard Oil, solid black with a large white "S."

The bulk of tonnage is limestone, iron ore taconite pellets, grain and coal, and steel. Most of it is carried in the familiar low-slung lakers, some of them equipped with the distinctive grids of self-unloaders, some dependent on the loading and unloading equipment at their ports of call.

But the most romantic sights are the deep-sea ships from around the world that are appearing with increasing frequency since the St. Lawrence Seaway's capacity for larger ships was increased. The salt-water craft are easy to spot. The lakers have pilot house and crew quarters in the bow, with the stack and engine at the stern. Those from

At Ludington State Park, the soul sinks in azure depths,
and is at peace.

Daisies challenge the rock-bound austerity of Lake Huron, near Detour.

68

overseas have the high bows to deal with hurricanes and typhoons, the bridge and stack amidships, and a low fantail.

They fly the flags of several dozen nations over their salt-encrusted hulls . . . the Marus from Japan, with loads of Toyotas, sake, steel, cameras, television sets and other imports that are a source of deep concern to American manufacturers. Newsprint from Finland and Norway and West Germany. Vodka from the USSR and Poland. Shoes and furniture from Italy. Wine from France. Electric switches and transistors from Taiwan. Mutton from Australia. Beef from Argentina. Thistle seed for American bird feeders from India and Ethiopia.

More than 4,000 deep-sea freighters enter the Seaway yearly, bound for Montreal, Quebec, Toledo, Buffalo, Detroit, Chicago, Duluth and Milwaukee. With their exotic cargoes; their crews leaning over the rails, talking in dozens of strange tongues; their flags faded by the suns of the China Sea, the Indian Ocean, the Persian gulf, they are Michigan's window to the world.

Foreign shipping had been coming to the Great Lakes a long time before the smaller canals and locks of the St. Lawrence were expanded into the present Seaway in 1959 to accommodate full-size freighters. The first foreign vessel to make the journey was the Madeira Pet, a 123-ton British brig that, in 1857, took 80 days to arrive at Chicago's North Pier.

The Chicago Board of Trade celebrated the event as the most important in the city's history. There was a city-wide celebration with much alternate band-playing of "Hail Columbia" and "God Save the Queen." The Pet departed amidst much international good feeling, with a load of salted hides and calf skins. It was the beginning of more than seven million tons of foreign freight to the Great Lakes yearly.

Until the Seaway's capacity for large ships was developed, big foreign freighters unloaded at Montreal. The new Seaway changed all that. It was one of the world's largest construction projects. Several miles of the new canal were of rock so hard it had to be heated with blow torches before a drill could cut into it for blasting.

The canals at Sault Ste. Marie were difficult, too. The first was at the Soo in 1797, and was the first lock in America. It was only 38 feet long, with a nine-foot lift, and served to get boatloads of furs from Lake

Superior to Lake Huron. It still exists as a memento of the past, although it had to be rebuilt.

With the development of the copper and iron ore finds along Lake Superior, something more elaborate was necessary. Construction of the present Soo Canal began on the Fourth of July of 1853, and it opened in 1855. There were two locks, each 350 feet long. Between them ships were raised 18 feet.

The locks and the "Miracle Mile" canal were completed none too soon. Many historians credit the Union victory in the Civil War to the iron that came through them in volume to make the cannon and shot, the military bridges, the Springfield rifles and the rest of the material of war that served the North all the way from the first Bull Run to Appomattox Courthouse.

There are now many locks at the Soo, the longest 1,200 feet, completed since World War II. The earlier locks, of which there were four in the early '40s, supplied the raw materials for Detroit, the Arsenal of Democracy, and may well have tipped the balance between the Allies and the Axis.

Besides cargoes of raw sugar from Central America and oil from Venezuela, Michigan's window to the world has been open on French, British and Polish warships, combat-scarred, making their weary way along the lakes for repair and refitting, a reminder that the world out there is dangerous, as well as romantic.

(Following Page) The wave thunder rarely dies down on Lake Huron in Alcona County.